The Devil's
No. 6

THE SUSAN ZETTLER STORY

The Date Now Is August 2019

LARRY ZETTLER

PAGE PUBLISHING, INC.
Conneaut Lake, PA

First originally published by Page Publishing 2021

ISBN 978-1-6624-0752-9 (pbk)
ISBN 978-1-6624-0753-6 (digital)

Printed in the United States of America

My name is Larry Zettler, and my wife's name is Susan Zettler. We have been married for the past forty-eight years, but for the past twenty years, my wife has had nothing but bad luck. The only way her luck could have been this bad is, the devil has had to play a big part in it. And I think he is going to give up, because she is still here, and he is not going to get her. In the following stories, you will find that they have accidents, crime, and poor medical issues that should of never happened. We live in a small town in Illinois. Population is 2,100 people. The town is Sesser, Illinois, about seventy miles east of St. Louis, Missouri. We are blessed with two daughters and two sons, fourteen grandchildren, and two great-grandchildren. All four of our children wouldn't trade their mom or granny for anything. And our grandchildren feel the same. Our great-grandchildren don't know her yet; they are too young. They all think she is about it. I just don't understand why she has had to go through this if I could have made it happen. I would have gone through everything for her. My wife would not hurt anyone, and she would help everyone.

Her bad luck started on the date of 6/6/96 in a 1996 Mercury Cougar. Also, the no. 6, I said, is the Devil's number. On this day, we were having a flashflood. My wife was on her way back from Pinckneyville, Illinois. She went to her mother's house on this day. She also went to see her mom once a week in Pinckneyville which is about seventeen miles from Sesser, Illinois. On this day, it was raining very hard, and the roads all had water standing on them in places. It was very hard to see while driving. A woman and her son were heading home toward Pinckneyville, Illinois. About three miles from Sesser, the woman and her son hit my wife head-on. There was also a car behind the car that hit my wife; they was also involved in the accident, and she was also from Pinckneyville. She is the only one that saw the accident. The first woman hit my wife head-on. I owned an auto repair shop and towing service in Sesser. The police called my service for towing; I was called by the police, and they told me to get to the accident but don't bring my tow truck. I then knew something wasn't right. So I got in my pickup and went to the accident scene. When I arrived, I saw three cars, and one car was my wife's car. I got out of my truck and ran to my car. I really thought she was dead. She was talking some. She had marks all over her face from the airbags. Her legs were pinned under the dash, and the steering wheel was against her chest. The fireman was cutting her out of the car. I was holding her hand to try to calm her down. The ambulance service arrived. They came over and checked her out and said she should be on a helicopter on her way to St. Louis. They called for her to be flown to St. Louis, but they said it was storming too bad. The ambulance said they would take her to St. Louis, but she needed to go to a hospital in Du Quoin, Illinois, first to get her stable. Then they would take her to St. Louis. Our kids followed in a car to St. Louis. When we arrived at St. Louis University Hospital, they took her right into the ER. Our youngest son worked at this hospital in the ER, but he wasn't working that night. He did meet us at the hospital. I think, since our son worked at the hospital, they took real good care of her. The doctor in the ER told us to wait in the waiting room. He said he would be in and tell us the details and what he needed to do to her. He came back in and told us what injuries she had and what he was going to have to do. He said she had a broken arm and two broken legs, with her femur bone out of her leg. Both ankles were crushed, and there were burns on her face from the airbag. He said he would come back in and tell us when he was going to do all this. He came back in a while later and told us what he was going to do and when. He said he was going to get some sleep and be back around five o'clock the next morning.

All four of our kids stayed the night in St. Louis and came back early the next morning. That morning, the Doctor said we could go in and see her before the surgery for just a few minutes. He sent us all down to the waiting room. He also said he would keep us updated on how the surgery was going. They did keep us updated. When the surgery was over, he told us that her ankles were not good and she would probably have problems with them. He told us to go and eat and we could come back and see her later on after we ate lunch. The doctor told us everything he did to her. He said they had to put rods, nuts, and bolts in her legs. Her ankles were the major part of the surgery. He said they were pretty bad. He said he had to rebuild both of them. He also said the ankles would probably cause more problems than anything. He said she will have problems and that she will probably limp a lot and, for sure, she won't be able to run. They also had to put a rod in her arm. St. Louis kept my wife for about a week. On the day that they were discharging her, they told her they found her a place to stay and get therapy and nursing done. They said she would have to stay about three months.

The next morning, we found out the place was in Carbondale, Illinois. It is about thirty miles from our house, and this was fine, and she was ready to go. They picked her up in an ambulance that morning to take her. I followed them in my car. They arrived at the nursing home parking lot in Carbondale. It looked nice. They took her inside the place into a room. When we got to the room, I'm sorry that I feel this way, but there was an old woman in the room that had the death raddles. I couldn't handle this; I know she felt the same way. I told them to load her back in the ambulance because she is not staying here. One of the nurses in the room asked me what the problem was, and I told her and that I was sorry I felt this way. They called the home's head person and told her what was wrong. She told them to put her in a room by herself. The room they put her in was nice and clean. She was okay with it. The next night, in the first room they put her in, the old woman that was in the room died. I told the nurse that I was sorry about last night when I lost my cool. They said that was no problem. They were all nice people and very helpful. My wife was here for three months. I drove every day after work to the nursing home for three months. While she was in the nursing home, an ambulance took her to St. Louis about three times. After this, I had to take her to St. Louis. The nursing home showed us how to do this. We didn't have any problems getting her in and out of the car.

The day finally came when they told her she could go home. When we got home, nurses came in about three times a week to check on her. They also had people come in and give her therapy. After about a month after she got back home from Carbondale, they had her walking some, and a rod in her leg broke. I finally got her to the car and took her back to St. Louis. She was there for a day and night. They told us the rod they put in was defective. They put another rod in and sent her home the next day. I was really surprised that we didn't have trouble getting her out of the house and in the car to go to St. Louis, but it went fine. The night she stayed at St Louis, I went in the waiting room, and I was lucky I got a place to sit. It was full. I fell asleep in the chair, and some woman woke me and said, "Mister, can you quit snoring? We can't get no sleep." I just got up and went outside the rest of the night. After the accident, she has had nothing but problems. This time, the state police got a hold of me and asked me if they could take pictures of our car so people can see how seat belts work and airbags can save your life. One other thing about the car accident, now I have two drivers and no passenger. My wife is always telling me to slow down or watch the car in front of me. This accident happened on the date of _6/6/96_ in a _1996_ Mercury Cougar. She still has problems with her ankles.

The devil didn't get my wife, but he sure tried. He sure messed her body up with all kinds of problems. We also had full coverage insurance, and so did the other car. The insurance paid one hundred thousand dollars, and that wasn't near enough to pay all the bills. We didn't think there would be any problems with the medical bills, but we were wrong. My wife had a therapy nurse that came to our house for about two months. After the auto accident, my wife got a sore on her leg, and it would not go away. I took her to a medical doctor just for this. We went to this doctor about six times, and she couldn't do my wife any good. So this doctor made her an appointment to see a doctor in a hospital at Mt. Vernon, Illinois. I took her for this appointment. The first thing this doctor did to my wife was, she asked her to walk for her. The doctor saw her limping and told her that she was going to fix this limp for her. The leg she limps on wasn't even the leg she had the sore on. She never did look at the leg she was having a problem with. We just walked out of the room. We never did find out about this problem. The sore finally went away. I tried to think of what it could be, the rod in her leg that she was allergic to it. Or the blood flow to her legs and feet. But I am not a Doctor.

Ten years after the auto accident, we bought a 2006 Chevy Impala S/S. It was a real nice car. But it seemed that this car ran too fast for us. This got us in a lot of trouble a few times. Again, the devil wanted my wife or the car. The way this story goes, about the 2006 Impala—this car gave us all kinds of bad luck when we owned it. We were in St. Louis, Missouri, in a parking garage. We didn't think about someone taking our license plate. We thought maybe it might get a dent in it.

A few days later, my wife was behind the car, and she noticed the license plate didn't look right. She walked around to the front of the car and looked at the plate, then walked to the rear again. She noticed the plate on the rear was different. Someone in St. Louis in the parking garage switched our rear plate with a plate off another car. This problem gave us a real big problem.

I drove the car for a few days before I did anything about the license-plate problem. Two weeks after someone switched our plate, we received a ticket from St. Louis police for running a stoplight. We have never been in this part of St. Louis. I didn't think too much about it, because you always hear about someone getting a ticket in the mail for this kind of problem. But after getting this ticket in the mail, we received three more for the same problem. This made four tickets. I already had two tickets. They were tickets from the Illinois State Police. They were warning tickets. After we received the tickets from St. Louis, I decided I needed to talk to someone about this problem. I went to the Sesser City Hall and told the police chief what was going on. I was then police commissioner in Sesser. The police chief told me that he would call St. Louis Police for me and have them send pictures of my car running the stoplight. He said he would call me when he got them. He called me in a couple of days and said he had them. I looked at the pictures, and it really did look like my car. I even thought it was my car, but I knew it wasn't. The policeman said to me, "That is your car. Unless you can prove it's not your car, you better stay away from St. Louis, because if you get caught there, you will be in real trouble." I looked the pictures over real good. I told the police chief again that it wasn't our car. I took the pictures with me and compared them to my car, and I could not find any difference in them. A day or so later, a State Policewoman came to my garage, and I told her about it. She said she would see what she could do for us. She came to my shop to check on some cars that I towed in for them. So she called State Police Headquarters and talked to them about it. I heard her say, "Oh my god, you got to be kidding me," then hung up the phone. She looked at me and said, "You are wanted in St. Louis County by the police for running a stoplight on different days, and not only that, you are wanted for armed robbery in St. Louis," and then she said there was nothing she could do to help me. I did show her the pictures and a picture of our car and said she couldn't tell the difference: "It sure looks like your car." She said, "The only thing you can do is prove it is not your car." She also said, "You have to keep looking at the cars until you can tell the difference." She told me, "You better stay away from St. Louis until you get this taken care of. The police don't know who you are there, and it is possible you could get shot up there because they don't care." I kept looking at the pictures and could not see any difference. I was really getting worried about this. I started looking at the pictures every day, and I could not find any difference at all. I decided I was going to St. Louis and talk to the police. The day I was going, I looked at the pictures one more time, and I finally found the problem: the place where we bought the car had a much-smaller decal than the other car; ours had the place it was bought at. Both stickers on the two cars had the stickers in the same place. The sticker on the other car was about four times the size ours was. I sent the pictures of our car and the other car to St. Louis Police, and they dropped the charges. With the Chevy Impala, I received four tickets from the St. Louis Police and two from the Illinois State Police. This made a total of _6_ tickets with this car.

Up until now, I thought I would write about something that was actually funny. So I can say life does have a few things that let you take your mind off all the bad things that happen. One day, my wife and I was at the Wal-Mart store in Benton, Illinois. We pulled into the parking lot in a parking spot. My wife just happened to see a big bottle of Tide wash soap on a concrete pole. There wasn't no car sitting around us. She said to me that she was going to get out of the car and see if the bottle was full. She checked, and it was full. She then said to me, "Do you think I will get in trouble if I put it in the car?" I told her, "They have video cameras on the light poles, but they never look at them." I said, "Besides that, if you don't take it, someone will probably take it, or take it back in the store and resale it." My wife worried about taking the Tide if she was going to get in trouble for it. After about a week, I have a Policeman in Sesser that I was really good friends with. I called him and asked him if he could do something for me. And he said yes. I asked him if he would call my wife and tell her the Wal-Mart store in Benton called the Benton Police Department and they have it on video her taking a big bottle of Tide from the parking lot. They said they wanted the Tide back or they would have her arrested. I told him what I wanted him to do, and he said he would. He called her and told her who he was and said to her that Benton Police called him to have her take the bottle of Tide back to Wal-Mart or they would arrest her. She then called me, and I asked her what was going on. She told me I needed to take her to Wal-Mart in Benton or they would have to arrest her. She was really scared. I then had to tell her this was a joke, but she didn't really believe it was a joke. I finally convinced her it was a joke, and she didn't think too much of this joke. She knew John, the cop from Sesser that called her. She talked to him and told him his time is coming. I have told everyone I know about this. And after I told her John was the cop that called her, she knew it was a joke. I have one more joke I will tell, then I will get back to the story *The Devil's No 6*.

John, the cop that I put up to calling my wife, was at my repair shop. He bought an older Dodge pickup, and the front end would make all kinds of noise when he turned the steering wheel. It was about to drive him crazy. The ball joints were bad on the front end.

I told him I could cut the rubber boots on them just a little and sprayed oil on them. I told him that this might help some until you can get them replaced. He drove it around the block, and it still made some noise, but not as bad. He asked if I could do anything else. I told him, "No, you need the ball joints changed." I said, "John, you need to take the truck out to Sesser Lake and drive the front end in the lake." I told him the water might help. He said, "Are you kidding me?" I said, "No, you know I wouldn't kid you." About thirty minutes later, he called and said, "Come out to Sesser Lake and pull me out." I got off the phone with him and thought to myself, *He is getting me back for telling him to do this.* When I got there, his truck's front end was really in the lake. I told him I was just kidding him. He thought I was serious. I pulled him out of the lake, and he told me, "Don't tell anyone about this." I said, "John, you know I wouldn't do that." By the next day, half the people in Sesser knew what he did. He also told his wife, and she said to him, "John, you know better than to do what he tells you." John is a great guy; his only problem: he is Polish.

One summer day, in April 2014, my wife brought me dinner to my shop. She was telling me about two young guys walking around our neighborhood, looking over fences, and walking in people's yards. She asked me if I could call the police and see if they could check them out. She said she has never seen them before. I called the police, but they were busy. They said it would be about an hour before they could check them out. So I went down, but I didn't see them. I told her they must have left town. I was still the police commissioner in town when I found out later that one of the guys lived just a block from us. My wife went back home, and I told her to call me if she saw them again. About two hours later, our neighbor across the street called me at work and told me to call the Police and get to her house as fast as I can. I had no idea what was wrong. I jumped in my tow truck and got there as quick as I could. I was probably running seventy miles per hour through town. When I got to her house, I saw the chief's police car at the neighbor's house. I parked in my driveway to keep it out of the road. I knew something was bad, wrong, but I didn't know what. I got out of my tow truck and ran over to the neighbor's house across the street. I opened her door and saw what was going on. My wife was laying on the floor with one of my work coats around her neck. I saw that she had her throat cut from ear to ear. I was in shock. I guess I didn't know what I was doing. The Police Chief told me to hold my coat tight against her neck. I was scared to death. The Police Chief kept telling me to hold the coat tighter. This was a very bad thing to help with, but when it is your wife, you got to do what you got to do. The only thing she said to me was that she loved me. This really got to me because of the shape she was in. I didn't think she would make it. The Sesser Fire Department arrived and got her loaded up in the ambulance. They had a helicopter waiting at a church by my auto shop. It landed in the parking lot. They loaded her into the helicopter and headed to St Louis. I stayed back out of the way of everyone. I was watching them. I started crying and couldn't stop. Several people came up to me and tried to calm me down. This had to be one of the worst days of my life by far. I am sure it was my wife's worst day also. I just didn't know what to think about what happened. I have been on several wrecker calls that were bad, but not like this. This was really like a nightmare.

My oldest son came, and before we went to the church parking lot, we locked our house up. Our son and both daughters and son-in-law got in my son's truck and drove to St. Louis University Hospital. On our way to St. Louis, the Illinois State Police was calling us, asking questions. I just thought about our car. I asked my son if he remembered seeing our car in the driveway, and he said no. So he called the State Police and told them our car was gone also. The Police asked us what kind of car it was and what color and year the car was. They also wanted to know if it had on star. We said yes, but we didn't have it working. They said, "That's OK. We can still use it." The car they stole was the 2006 Chevy Impala. On the way to St. Louis, we still didn't know what happened to her. All I could think about was what I would do if she didn't make it.

Our youngest son, Jeff, worked at this Hospital, but he was off that day, although he did meet us there. He worked in the ER, and they all took good care of her. They took her into the ER when we got there. They told us the Doctor would come and talk to us and told us to wait in the waiting room. The doctor came in and said he was finished and she was OK. He also told us whoever did this to her, it was a good thing they didn't know what they were doing. By now there were several cops from Illinois. There they asked us about what happened, and we told them we didn't know. I did tell them early in the day that she told me that there were two boys walking around, looking over fences and in people's yards. She asked me if the cops could go down and see what they wanted. I went, and she stayed at my shop while I went to see, but I didn't see them anywhere around. By now there were several police from Illinois at the hospital asking about what happened, but we didn't know. They got a call a little later and said they caught the guys that did this. "On star" in our car led the police to them. They were in Mt. Vernon, Illinois. The doctor told us we could go in and see her when she wakes up. He said she needs her sleep now. The State Police waited also. Why, she got some sleep.

When she woke up, I went in the room to see her. I asked her if she felt like talking to the State Police, and she said yes. I went and asked the doctor if it would be OK for her to talk to them, and he said yes, just as long as they didn't stay long. I had them come in her room. They were very nice to her. She told them that the White boy knocked on the door and wanted to know if they could use her phone to talk to their mom. She told them, "In about fifteen minutes," because she was talking to her mom. They did come back in fifteen minutes and knocked on the door. She went to the door and opened it to hand them the phone when she did this. The White boy jerked the door open and hit her with his fist and knocked her out in the floor where my coats hung. This all happened on our rear porch. They went through everything. They took her purse, which had a little money. She said, "Around sixty dollars," she thought. But the car key was in her purse. The car key was what they wanted so they could go to Mt. Vernon; we had the 2006 Chevy Impala. She didn't know how long they were in the house. When they were on their way out, my wife was still in the floor where they knocked her out. The colored boy on the way out must have taken one of our kitchen knives and cut her throat on the way outside. My wife said she remembered the colored boy doing this because he had her by the hair and lifted her head up then cut her throat. We didn't ever know this, but the White boy just lived a block from us. They kept my wife for a couple of days in the hospital after this before she could go home.

When we got back home to Sesser, our storm door was missing. The State Police took it for fingerprints. The car was also gone; they took it for fingerprints. Our neighbors across the street also cleaned up our house inside on the floor and the things the boys did in the house. When we got home, our kids got together and bought a new patio set for our rear deck. People took up collections and benefits for her and sent her money. They sent money in the mail also. I don't remember if I even thanked people for what they did. Everyone was great, and we are very sorry if we didn't. I know it was a while before we got our heads together. The people that live in Sesser are all great, caring people. Till this day, people ask me how my wife is doing. The day after we got back home, my wife wanted to go to the Police Station and thank the Chief of Police for what he did. A lot of people said that he saved her life, and I also think that he did. He is one of the best EMTs around; anyone would tell you this. She had to hug him. She also wanted to thank our neighbors, and she did. They were the neighbors that cleaned our house for us. I think about everyone in town started locking their doors and windows, even people in other towns around. I had nightmares after this for a while also. My nightmares were about someone standing over me and I couldn't move. I would also wake up in the middle of the night and check all the doors and windows to see if they were locked. I couldn't imagine what my wife was going through. After this happened, I wasn't going to let anyone else hurt her.

Our oldest son is the General Manager in the Chevy dealership in Benton, Illinois. The State Police called him and said he could come after our car. They said they were done with it. He sent a tow truck after it. He called me and said the car was ready. He had it cleaned up for us also. When he got it done, he called me and told it was ready. He asked me if I needed him to come after me. I told him no; someone was here to get it. When I got a ride to the dealership, I went in and got the keys. He did have it all cleaned up; it looked new. I talked to him for a little while. I told him I better get back home and see if she was OK. We both are very proud of him to have a job like he has, and he is good at it. I got in our car and checked everything to see if it was OK. I then looked at the odometer, and it showed _66,666_ miles. I took the keys back to my son and told him I didn't want it any longer, and he asked why. I said to him, "Go out and start it, then look at the odemeter, and you will see why." I really did not want to get rid of it, but I had to. He came back in and told me he didn't blame me. This is, without a doubt, the devil's numbers. We really hated to get rid of this car, but it was, for sure, a bad-luck car for us.

Until this day, people that see me always ask about my wife. My wife is doing better, but this incident with the boys, she will never get over it. We went to court over this probably ten or fifteen times before they sentenced them for prison time. The guys were in court one day, and a woman that was sitting behind me said something about the colored boy. The brother was sitting a couple of rows in front of us and turned her way and told her she better shut up. The judge said he would clear the courtroom if something like this happens again. They sentenced them to thirty-five years, and they had to serve eighty percent of their time before a chance for parole. I heard from some prison employees that the Black boy made a deal with Feds that he would wear a tape recorder in Drew Peterson's cell and get him to talk about killing his wives and he got the information they needed. Drew Peterson was the Chicago cop that killed two of his wives, and he would not talk to the Feds. I would say that the colored boy was wanting to shorten his sentence, but they said the judge wouldn't do it. I do know, if the judge in Franklin County was the judge, he wouldn't lessen his time at all. I don't know about a different judge. If they do let him out sooner, he better never come around Sesser, Illinois, again because people around here will sentence him themselves. I hate to keep calling him a Black boy, but he is just a boy. To me, the White boy is just as guilty. I always heard that prisoners didn't like snitches, and I hope that he finds this out if he is in or out of prison. The two boys that did this messed up their lives for a long time. The things I have told you so far are only about half of the things that have happened to my wife. Everything is very true.

Thanksgiving Day in 2014, my wife had a problem slurring her words. I didn't do anything because I wanted to make sure that I was right. The next morning, her speech was worse. I called our kids and told them what I was going to do. I put her in the car and took her to the ER in Mt. Vernon, Illinois. The ER Doctor asked me what was going on with her. I told him, "Her speech, she is slurring her words." He checked a few things and said he could not find anything. He sent her back home. The next morning, she had the same problem. But it was worse this time. I took her to Mt. Vernon ER again. The same doctor was working in the ER again. The doctor again said he couldn't find anything again. He sent her back home again. This time, I was starting to get very upset with them, and there was a different ER doctor. I told this doctor that this makes the third time in three days. I wanted something done. I told the doctor, "If this hospital can't find anything wrong, send her somewhere that can." He asked me if she has had a mental problem in the past. I said, "No, but the things she has been through in the past, it wouldn't surprise me." The ER Doctor called someone in to look at her. He said she was having seizures. He didn't give her any kind of test to see if this was the problem. I didn't go for his answer. I have seen people having seizures before, and this wasn't the problem. He did seem like a smart doctor, but I think he was fake. Now we had a choice to go with the doctor or see someone for a mental problem. This doctor also gave her meds for the seizures, but we didn't use it. So I told the ER doctor we wanted her to get checked for a mental problem. I asked the ER doctor if he could get her into a mental hospital to get her checked. He said, "No, they are all full." I said, "What are we going to do?" He said, "The only way you can get her in one is to go to our sister hospital in Centralia, Illinois. He said we have a mental ward there. You would have to take her there." They could check her there in the ER, and they would admit her. He also said, "Don't tell them you were sent by this Hospital." The ER there gave her all the same tests that Mt. Vernon ER gave her. I told the doctor at Centralia hospital she had done all of them at Mt. Vernon Hospital. They admitted her in the hospital to see if she did have a mental problem. That evening, when she was in her room, the doctor that was going to check her for this problem said he would check her later that evening. Also, the doctor from Mt. Vernon Hospital came in and told her he would also be back to check her for the seizures.

I left the Hospital around nine o'clock that night and came back the next morning, around 7:00 AM. When I got to the hospital, she was sitting on the bed with her clothes on. I asked her what she was doing. She told me she was discharged. I said to her, "You can't go home yet." She said, "The doctor said I could." I told her the two doctors that were in said they were going to check her, but she only talked to one doctor, and he checked for a mental problem. I asked her about the doctor from Mt. Vernon, and she said no. I told her I was going to talk to the nurse at the desk. I asked her why they discharged her. She said she didn't know. I said I would like to know what they found. She said, "You will have to call the doctor at his office in Mt Vernon." I did call the doctor's office in Mt. Vernon. They said, "You need to make an appointment to see him." I have never seen this before; you have to pay for him not doing anything, and we didn't get any answer from the hospital. The doctor's office in Mt. Vernon made an appointment for her, and she said we would have to bring one hundred dollars cash before he would talk to us. They set us up with an appointment for the next day, our kids.

My wife and I went to the appointment. We went into a room with the doctor. He said that she was having seizures. I told him, "You don't know that, you didn't even test her for this." And he said, "Yes, I did." The seizure doctor came out good on this deal. He made money from Centralia Hospital and one hundred dollars cash from us, and we ended up with nothing. Mt. Vernon Hospital was the same way. They made money for nothing. I told the quack doctor's nurse, "Your boss should be fired from this hospital." He still insisted that she was having seizures, and I told him he was crazy. I told this doctor, "You have said the whole time she was having seizures and didn't even test her for them." I told him he was full of s——. I told him, "If this hospital doesn't fire you soon, they are not going to have the money for all your problems. It is no wonder why a hospital has so many malpractice lawsuits with doctors like this." He also pre-scribed seizure medicine for her seizures, but I wouldn't let her take it. We took her back home. She seemed okay for now.

She felt good for about two weeks, but she got sick again. This time, when she got sick, it was worse than the other times. We took her back to Mr. Vernon Hospital. And I don't know why. I guess I thought one time out of four, they could do something right. I thought she might get a doctor this time that knew what he was doing. They took her up to a room in the hospital and not the ER. The doctor she had now, it seemed like he cared. It seemed like he knew what was going on. He wanted to find her problem. He put an IV in and gave her some medicine. She just kept getting worse.

Jeff, our youngest son, knew a doctor in St. Louis where he worked. Jeff called this doctor and told him about the things going on with her the last month. This doctor told Jeff to send him all the tests she has had at Mt Vernon. He said he would look at them. He said to Jeff he would call him back. If you have the right people on your side, you can get the medical records. The doctors in St. Louis looked them over. The doctor in St. Louis called Jeff back and told him he found her problem; she was having ministrokes. Jeff told the doctors at Mt. Vernon that she was having ministrokes, and the seizure doctor didn't know what to say about that. The doctor from St. Louis told Jeff what they needed to do. They did do it and found out the doctor in St. Louis was right. The doctors in St. Louis talked to the doctor in Mt. Vernon. The only bad thing is that the doctor that said she was having seizures was the doctor that was going to do this procedure. With all this Doctor did, I told the other doctors that I didn't want him to touch her again after he said she was having seizures. This makes the fourth time we had her at this hospital, and not one time did they ask what she was allergic to, and she is very allergic to three medicines. You might know this is the medicine she was allergic to.

The next morning, I got back to the hospital. I walked into her room, and she was red as a fire truck. One of the nurses said to me when I walked in, "Sir, we are very sorry, but we gave her a medicine she is allergic to." You could tell by the way she looked that she felt terrible. One of the nurses told me that they could give her a med-icine that would clear her up. I told her no. I said, "I have brought her in four times in a week, and if anything happens to her, I would be blamed for bringing her here. I will take her to her regular doctor because your hospital will kill her if I don't." She said, "I'll have to get her discharge papers for you to sign." I told her to take the discharge papers to the hospital administrator and wipe with them. I am very lucky I got her out of here while she can still talk. I asked the nurse who the doctor was that gave her this test. And it was the doctor that kept telling us that she was having seizures. I told them I didn't want this doctor touching her, but he did. He didn't have a clue what he is doing.

I took her to her regular doctor. He could not believe the way she looked. He said someone is going to be in big trouble over this. Her doctor called the meds in for her to take care of the reaction to the medicine for what the hospital gave her. It took her a couple of days to get over this. She also got her meds for her ministrokes after about a week she took the meds. The meds for the ministrokes, they really helped her. After a few days, we talked to a couple of attorneys, and they said, "We don't have a case against them." The next day, I called the hospital administrator at Mt. Vernon and told her a lit-tle about what happened. We made an appointment. It was in two weeks. They said they could talk to us then. We went to the appoint-ment with the hospital. I told them everything that happened in their hospital. "This is why we need to talk to you…" I told them that my wife was in the ER three times. They wanted to know what happened. I said my wife was in their hospital and had the worst service that anyone could have. I told them my wife was in their ER three days in a row and they didn't help her any. I also told them about the seizure doctor about how big of a fraud he was and that if they don't get rid of him, they are going to have more lawsuits than they can handle. They said they would get back with us.

They did tell us that they have had a few problems with him. I told them they haven't had any problems yet. The hospital adminis-trator called me back a week later. She asked me what we wanted. I told her we wanted *Centralia* Hospital. Bill dropped; they said they couldn't do this. They also said they couldn't take care of the times she was in the ER. I asked her why they couldn't take care of this. They then told me that the doctors in the ER don't work for them. She said that they were all contracted out. I then said to her, "You mean, you are not going to take care of anything." They said they were sorry. I told them, "Everything that was done, was done in your hospital." I said to her, "You must think we are stupid." I let a week pass, and they called me back and said they would take care of everything, and she said again they were sorry. We talked to two lawyers about this. They said they don't have cases like this. They told me, "You did a good job getting them to take care of the bills." If it wasn't for the doctor in St. Louis University Hospital, she wouldn't have even made it out of this hospital. The deal with Mt. Vernon Hospital was one big nightmare. I do think a lot of the blame was myself taking her back four times. But I sure didn't think we would have these problems.

About a month later, my wife got sick again and just kept getting worse by the day. This time, I took her to a hospital in Herrin, Illinois. She did like this hospital. They decided she had a heart problem. She was in intensive care. They were giving her a medicine for her heart. She started doing a little better with the heart medicine, until she ended up with MRSA. This is a very bad infection. They put her in a room by herself. You had to wear a mask and gown to go into her room. This made her very sick for about two weeks. After she was feeling better, they sent her back home. I still didn't feel like she was doing very good. But she was better than she was. After a couple of days, she was admitted back in the hospital. They said the MRSA was still making her sick. They kept her this time. She was there for about a week this time, then she was discharged again.

In the month of May 2016, I called her doctor to see him. He asked me what was wrong, and he said for me to bring her over now. After he checked her, he said, "You better take her to Mt. Vernon Hospital now." Her doctor also knew the problems she had before with Mt. Vernon Hospital. Since we were there the last time they had their new hospital finished, they had a lot of new doctors and nurses. I took her into the ER. They admitted her right into the ER. I sure hoped she didn't have a heart attack. They did a test for her heart and said she did have a problem. All our kids and son-in-law were there. They told us what they were going to try on her. They were going to try a procedure. This was to stop her heart and retime it. Our youngest son, Jeff, told us about the procedure they were going to do. He also said they have to have a doctor, nurse, and heart machine when they do this. They didn't do this until the next day.

The following morning, my brother and I were in her room, and a nurse came in. My wife was asleep. They did do the procedure, but they forgot what they were doing. The nurse came into the room. She gave her a shot in her IV. She didn't even talk to us; she just gave her the shot. As soon as she put the needle in my wife, she sat straight up in bed, her eyes turned white, and she fell back in her bed. The nurse just stood there. My brother called for a crash cart, and our son ran into her room. The doctor and some more nurses ran into the room also. They ran us out of the room, in the hall. I didn't know what to do. I had a come apart. The nurse in the room did not do anything. When I went out in the hall, I just broke down crying. My brother told the nurses in the hall to check my blood pressure. I told them, "I don't care right now about anything but my wife." I told them the nurse in her room killed her. The nurse in the hall told me I needed to go to the ER and get checked out. They thought I was having a heart attack. The doctor then came out and said I needed to go to the ER right now. I told him, "I am not going anywhere until I find out about my wife." They said she is going to be okay. I didn't go to the ER. I went outside. From what I understand, our youngest son, Jeff, ran in the room and gave her CPR. This is the only time I've ever seen someone die. And the bad part: it was my wife.

My daughter took me outside. I was outside for about forty-five minutes and told my daughter she could go back in, that I was okay. I stayed out for a few minutes longer then went inside. My brother also knew some things about the medical field. He was a fireman once; they did have things in situations like this. After I was outside for a while, I went back into the hospital. I saw the doctor in the hall, and he said I could go in and see her. I went back in her room, and she was sleeping. I stayed in her room for about an hour, and she was still asleep. I then went back outside to our car. I probably cried for an hour. I just couldn't quit. I am a person that just doesn't cry—I can't say that anymore. I went back inside again. I forgot my oldest son and oldest daughter came to the car and sat with me for a while. I went back inside the hospital to her room, and she was still asleep. I stepped out in the hall and saw our youngest son and son-in-law sitting in the waiting room. So I walked in and said, "I know you guys are big church people," and what I said next to them, I don't know where it came from. I told them, "I know you guys are big church people, but I have something to say to the both of you." They said, "What is it?" I said, "I know both of you guys are into church life. But I need to get something off my chest." They asked me, "What is it?" I said, "Both of you believe in God. I then said to them all the things, bad things, wouldn't have happened to her if there was a god. I said she wouldn't hurt anyone like she has been hurt. They said to me that there is a god and God has pulled through every time she was hurt. I told them as I was walking out of the room, "You guys can believe what you want, but if there was a god, this wouldn't have happened to her, not these many things." I told them I was sorry I said this to them. Later that day, we decided to get her flown to St. Louis, to get her out of there. I told them it seems like every time she has been to their hospital when she is sick, she will be sicker or dead when she leaves. A new hospital with new doctors and nurses... you would think it would be a good place to go. But I will tell you, it didn't work like this.

The helicopter flew her to St. Louis, and we started to. They had her in an intensive care unit when we arrived. This has been the worst she has ever been. And we didn't think she was going to make it. The next day, they gave her a lot of tests. All the doctors and nurses that were caring for her seemed to be good to her. On the third day, they took her out of her room to do a small surgery. I think it was to put another IV in her. We all waited until they brought her back to her room. We gave them time to get her hooked back up to things. We went back in her room.

When we went back into her room, they had her right hand bandaged up. They didn't tell us right then. They told us someone learning to be a doctor tore her artery into. This was a student from their medical school at the hospital. That day they moved her to another floor, they did not tell us they were going to move her to a different floor, and this wasn't an intensive care floor. After what they did to her, they should of never moved her to regular floor. I went up to the floor they transferred her to.

When I walked into her room, she was holding her hand and crying; you could tell she was really in a lot of pain. I asked her what was wrong. She said, "I need something for my hand. It hurts bad." I asked if she pushed the nurse's button, and she said, "Yes, for about thirty minutes." I then pushed it a few times, and they didn't come. I then told her I will get them in here. I was really mad. I said, "I am going out in the hall. I will get them in here fast." So I went in the hall. I was so loud the whole floor should have heard me. A nurse across the hall heard me and said, "Sir, I am busy." I said, "I see you are." I told her, "She needs pain meds." I thought they would have taken better care of her after this. I told the nurses that she is going to lose her fingers because of this hospital, and now they don't want anything to do with her. This is really something: a person comes in with heart problems, and they end up cutting your fingers off.

The next day, a plastic surgeon came in and looked at her fingers. She made her an appointment to get her fingers taken care of her right hand. The plastic surgeon that was going take her fingers off was the only one in the hospital that said she was sorry that this happened to her. The next day, they sent her back to Southern Illinois, to Carbondale Illinois Hospital. Like I said, they didn't want anything else to do with her. One of the nurses that I got to come in to my wife's room to give her some pain meds, I saw her outside. Later she came over and said she was sorry again. I told her I wasn't sorry I said what I said. But you wouldn't believe what kind of service she has had in the hospitals she has been in so far. One hospital killed her, and this hospital cut the fingers off her right hand. And they didn't even say they were sorry. Carbondale, Illinois, is about thirty-five miles from Sesser, Illinois, where we live. The hospital at St. Louis, every time I would go outside, they would tell me how good this hospital was. I told them it sure wasn't good today for my wife.

The hospital in Carbondale had my wife flown in a helicopter to them. Carbondale is a heart hospital, and they are very good. The doctor in Carbondale checked her heart and said she needs heart surgery and a valve put in. He told us that he didn't want to do it because she was too big of a risk. He said she needs more than just a regular heart surgery. He called a doctor in Springfield. The doctor in Springfield told him he would do it. He said he has done three that had the same problem. The doctor in Carbondale made an appointment with the doctor in Springfield, Illinois, to see the heart surgeon. They checked her over real good. They told her she needs to get her fingers done first. We had to go up to St. Louis about three times for the surgery, once for the surgery and twice after. The surgeon for her fingers said she can go ahead and have the heart operation done; she released her. She was in Carbondale Hospital for a week. We should have come here first; they were good. They did more for her than any hospital did.

We called Springfield Hospital back for the heart surgery, and they told her in two weeks, about 3:00 PM. She needed to be there the day before the surgery. They also booked a room at a hotel across the street. That evening, I took her out to eat and showed her Springfield. We got to the room later in the day, and she was ready. As soon as we got to the room, she went to sleep. The next morning, we got to the hospital about 4:00 AM, and they took her right in. All four of our kids met us there. They drove all the way from Sesser, which is 175 miles.

They let us all go into the room. The doctor and nurse came in, asked her about the heart valve that needed to be replaced, they told us there were two choices on the valve: one was a mechanical valve, and the other, a pig valve. He said the difference was, with the mechanical valves, she would have to stay with meds for the rest of her life; the pig valve, she shouldn't have to. We said the pig valve, just as long as she doesn't start sounding like a pig; the doctor said he couldn't tell us that. The doctor told us all to wait in the waiting room. I forgot how long he said it would take. He said they would keep us informed on how things were going. It seemed like the surgery was taking forever. You think all kind of things that could go wrong. He finally came back in the waiting room and told us everything went well. He also said she needed her rest. He told us we should all go out to lunch somewhere. He said if something comes up, they would contact us. He assured us that he wouldn't have to call. After about a week, the doctor said she is ready to go home.

Later that afternoon, the social worker came in her room. He told us she is going to have to go to a rehab and nursing facility. He asked us if we had a place in mind. We told him Herrin Hospital in Herrin, Illinois, or somewhere in Benton, Illinois, which is only fifteen miles from our home. He told us he would check these places and get back to us today. But he never did. She could have gone home that evening if he could have gotten her a place to stay. He never came back that day. She was really wanting to go home. We waited all evening. He did come back the next day around noon. Both of us were getting pretty ticked off at him. I went back to the room that night. I came back to the hospital about six in the next morning. We waited the biggest part of the day for the social worker to come back in her room. He came to her room around 3:00 PM that day. He said he tried Herrin Hospital and Benton; he said they were full. However, he said he did find a place in Herrin; it was when you get to Herrin, it is on the left side of the road. I told my wife after he left, "I hope it's not the place I think it is." The social worker brought the papers to give to the nursing home. It was about 4:30 PM. Now, we were only two days late.

The doctor and his nurse came in the room to tell us bye. He had to leave pretty quick, but the nurse stayed for a little while. She told my wife, if we needed anything, to call her. She gave us her phone number for the hospital and her personal phone number. This nurse, you would have thought she was a relative or a good friend. She said to call, day or night. The bad thing about this was, it would probably never see her again. We got out of the hospital about 4:00 PM that evening on our way to Herrin.

It was now about 8:00 PM, at the nursing home I didn't want her to stay at. I did go, and as soon as I went in, I found out it was like we thought it was; it didn't look too clean. I went up to the nurses' desk to talk to the person in charge. I also took the discharge papers with me. I put them on the desk. About that time, I heard her say, "I am not staying here." I didn't know it, but two nurses went out a different door and pushed her in. In the room they took her to, there was an old lady in a bed that also had the death raddles. You know it's bad when you get put in a room like this. They were going to put her in here; it's not the old lady's fault. After what my wife's been through, she didn't need this. I went and got her and took her back to the car. The nurse asked me why we wouldn't stay there. I told her, "You should know what the problem is. It's dirty, and some of your people needed to take a bath." They were still trying to talk to me about keeping her. I told her, "Your help may be the best ever around, but your place is dirty." I said, "She will have to stay for three months, and it would take longer for you to clean this place up." I hated doing this; they all seemed to be real nice. The head nurse came out to the car and brought the discharge papers out and gave them to me. She did tell me she could get her into another place that the company owns. We said, "That's okay, we will pass on it."

The papers I took into the nursing home, the head nurse came out to the car and gave them to me. We were at the nursing home, and a nurse came out and told me there was a real good place on the other end of Herrin; it's Heli Care. It is real clean and a real nice place. We told her, "Thanks." She said, "Please don't tell anyone about this." She said she would get fired. I told her she didn't have to worry about that. It was now about 8:30 PM. I got to the other place in Herrin, and it was real nice. I went in, and an employee asked if she could help me. I told her our story. She said that they don't have anyone to check her in at Herrin. I told her she really needed a place to stay tonight. But I told her, if I get someone to give meds to her tonight, I would just take her home for tonight. She said she would have a person in charge call me the next morning. I told my wife we will go to Herrin Hospital; they should do it.

We went to Herrin Hospital. I got out of the car and told her I would be right back. I needed the discharge papers from Springfield to let them know what kind of meds she needed. I couldn't find the papers. I told her we were going back to the nursing home. They didn't have anyone to check her in at Herrin Nursing Home until morning. I told her she really needed a place tonight, but I told her if I could find someone to give her meds to her this morning, I would just take her home. She said she would have the person in charge call me. I told my wife we will go to the Herrin ER. They should do it there.

So we went to the Herrin ER. I got out of the car and told her I will be right back. I needed the discharge papers from Springfield. I couldn't find the papers. I told my wife, "I must have left them at the first place we stopped at." We got back to the nursing home. I went back in and asked the nursing home, but they didn't have them. It was now 11:30 PM, and I was getting very upset, and I know she was really tired. I really didn't want to go back there, but I had no choice. So we got back there. I asked them if I left the papers from Springfield on their desk; they looked and said no. I said I guess I lost them. I said I was going to look in their drive and ditch. They brought flashlights out and helped me look, but we couldn't find them. I said I'll just go back to Herrin ER and see if they would do it without the papers, and I found them on the road.

We went back to the ER. I saw something. I told them about our problems. I told her, the social worker at Springfield Hospital, where she wanted to stay for a while. "But you were booked up. She needed nursing and therapy for three months." I told the nurse that he checked here first. "But you were full at the time. I told her I need someone to give her meds to her." I also told her about the nursing home she didn't want to stay at. The charge nurse told me, "Sir, we don't have Therapy Department in this hospital." I said, "What do you mean you don't have a Therapy Department here?" I told her my wife has been here for therapy. She said it again. I told her, "I don't think that you know what you are talking about." I said, "Besides, she doesn't need therapy. She needs someone to give her meds to her. That is on the papers. I've got them here. And that is all we needed." She then told me, "Sir, we don't keep meds in this hospital." It was a real bad thing for her to say this. I lost it. I called her anything I could think of and much more, and it wasn't nice. Then the nurse told me, "Why don't you take her back where she didn't want to stay?" I told the nurse, "If you were a man, I would pull you out of there, and the fight would have been on." I then said, "The best thing for you to do is just shut your mouth or I will pull you out of there and make you eat the things you said. Matter of fact, you don't have to be a man. You need the hell beat out of you so you can't talk any more." I then was escorted out of the ER with a couple of security police. She was a real b——h. They shouldn't let someone like her work around people. The last few years has really changed me. I would have never said what I did to anyone. I have bad temper now, and it is getting worse.

I think, so far, this was the worst day and night of my life. I got back in the car. She asked me what was wrong. I said, "Please don't talk to me right now. I'll tell you in a little while." Our oldest son called me also, and I gave the phone to my wife so she could talk to him. On this day/night, I just felt so worthless. I couldn't help her at all. I finally did talk to my son. Then he asked me what I was going to do. He also told me I needed to cool down before I have a heart attack. That would be the easy way out. I then told him, "I am just going to take her back to Springfield. I've had enough."

Springfield is about two hundred miles from Herrin. I started on our way back to Springfield and got about two miles out of Herrin. I told her, "I think I will go to Carbondale Hospital and see what they say." We got to the hospital and drove up to the ER, and one of the security people came to the car, and he did this so fast I couldn't tell him what the problem was. He took her on into the ER. When I got into the ER, I told them what the problem was; they said they would do it for us.

After she got out of the ER, it was six thirty in the morning. We got her home. Our son met us at our house. He helped me get her in the house. As soon as we got back home, she laid down and went to sleep. The time now was seven thirty. I stayed up and called some places about getting her a place to stay. I would never go through a night like this again. I told the ER about the things that happened to us. They couldn't believe what happened to us. They couldn't believe what happened at Herrin. This is Carbondale's sister hospital. The ER doctor said to us that someone will get in big trouble over this. I called the hospital administration about the nurse at Herrin ER. She said she would check it out and see what happened and take action if needed. I bet she didn't do anything.

The nursing home from Herrin called me this morning. She said, "We have a place in Benton," but I will have to have a letter from the social worker at Springfield. I told her, "I will call him then call you back." I called the social worker. And they told me he wasn't in his office; they said he will call me back. I called the nursing home back and told her he wasn't in his office and would call me back. It was now about 3:00 PM, and he never did call me back. It was getting late in the afternoon, and he never did call. The gal at the nursing called us back. I didn't know what to tell her. She said, "Just bring her over, and I will admit her." This place was Helia Nursing Home, in Benton, Illinois. I took her over to Benton at the nursing home. They showed her around, and she told me that this place was good. It was a nice, clean place, and all the staff was good.

After I took her to the nursing home and had her admitted, I then came back home while they were getting her settled in. I was thinking about what the heart doctor's nurse said to us: "If you need something, just call her." So I called her, and she was at work at the hospital. I got her answering machine; she said she would return the call, and she did in about ten minutes. I told her who I was, and she asked me how my wife was doing. She asked me what I needed, and I told her what we had been through and about the social worker not calling me back. She said, "Give me about thirty minutes," and she would call me back. I waited, and she called back in about thirty minutes. She told me she got everything taken care of. She said she got her checked into the nursing home and found the social worker, and she also got his attention. She said she also talked to the nursing home. I couldn't thank the heart doctor's nurse for what she did for us. I told her that the next time we were in Springfield, we were going to take her out for dinner. I hated to bother her at work; she said that was no bother. She said, "Call again if you need to." She got everything that I told her we needed. She said the social worker's ears were really burning now. But she didn't care. This nurse was very, very special to the both of us. The social worker called me and said he got everything all set for my wife. I told him, "You didn't do anything. The nurse that worked with the heart doctor did everything. She was a real good person because you didn't do anything."

The wife was in the nursing home for three months. And she was ready to go home four months after the heart surgery. The wife wasn't doing to good. She was watching TV. She yelled for me. She said she couldn't breathe. She really was in bad shape. I didn't even think that she was having a heart attack after she had major heart surgery done on her. I called 911. They asked me all kinds of questions. A lot of them didn't make sense. I asked the 911 operator to call Sesser Fire. I told them I needed someone here now. They then called Franklin County EMS. The dispatch service called the Franklin Co. EMS. This dispatch called me and asked me what kind of problem she was having. I said she was having a heart attack. The EMS operator then called. I told them to just get someone here now. They just kept asking questions. I finally hung up, but before I hung up, I told them I had to get off the phone. "You can ask me these questions later." They made it over here and said she was having a heart attack. They took her to be hospital and checked her out. They then had her sent to Carbondale by ambulance.

Carbondale found out that she had a heart blockage, so they had to put a stint in her. My wife just had open-heart surgery. You wouldn't think after open-heart surgery she would have this problem. I didn't believe in the devil, but if his number is 6, what can you say? We still have doctor's appointments three times a month or more. She has been in the hospital six times since the heart surgery and probably ten times before the heart surgery. After the heart surgery after the last heart attack, she had to go to Herrin Hospital for three months, three times a week for therapy. About five months ago, she was on the couch having problems breathing. I told her I was going to take her to the Carbondale ER, and she didn't want to go. But I talked her into going to the hospital. I ran every stoplight. I was running around seventy miles per hour right through these small towns. I also ran every light in Carbondale. We made it okay. When we usually go through these small towns, we didn't see police around. I was kind of hoping one would stop me so they could get in front of us. Carbondale Hospital had to put another stint in her. This is the second time since the heart surgery. With all the problems she has had, the devil has had to play a part in it.

My wife's mother died on my birthday, 2/19. She also had two brothers die and a younger sister the last seven years. One of her brothers was born on 5/19/51. They are one year apart. There was a total of _6_ in the family. They are all gone except for her. Her brothers and sister all passed away in their <u>sixties</u>. There was Dad, Mom, two brothers, sister, and my wife. If you think about it, my wife has had bad things that have happened to her, but the devil has still not gotten her. When my wife has been in the hospitals as much as she was, not one of her brothers or sister came and saw her. Everything that I wrote about is 100 percent true; you probably don't think it is. But I would never write about this if it wasn't true. I just wanted people to know that my wife is still her. Everything but the Herrin ER when the charge nurse was let out of her cage... But it is true; I just can't prove it. Before this all happened, I would never had an outburst like this. I will tell you, it feels pretty good to do it, get it off your chest. Some of the things that have happened to my wife were probably my fault, like the times I took her to Mt. Vernon Hospital.

The auto repair shop that I owned in Sesser for forty-five years, when my wife got sick, I had it closed when she was in all the different hospitals. I missed so much work that I didn't have money coming in. I also lost my interest in it. When I did work, I could be working on a car, but I would just start crying. This business was my pride and joy for the forty-five years that I owned it. But I just didn't want to look at the place any longer. I had an auction and sold everything. I should have given it away. I didn't make any money at all. I had about $150,000 dollars' worth of tools and $70,000 property and got $42,000. I just wanted to sell it and get away from it. Now I stay at home every day, and I just can't take it. I have done everything around our house that needed to be done. These past four years have really gotten to me. I used to hold everything in, but I don't any longer. I really lose my temper fast, and it actually feels good. I have seen my wife go through so much. I just can't take it. I know if I could find something to do, things will get better. Thank you for reading this. I hope it kept you on your toes, but believe this, it has had me on my toes for a while.

CPSIA information can be obtained
at www.ICGtesting.com
Printed in the USA
BVHW071730050821
613732BV00003B/442